POSITIONS ON THE TEAM

POSITIONS IN
SOCCER

EMMETT MARTIN

PowerKiDS press

New York

Published in 2023 by The Rosen Publishing Group, Inc.
29 East 21st Street, New York, NY 10010

Portions of this work were originally authored by Ryan Nagelhout and published as *Soccer: Who Does What?* All new material in this edition was authored by Emmett Martin.

Editor: Therese Shea
Book Design: Michael Flynn

Photo Credits: Cover (soccerball) irin-k/Shutterstock.com; (series jersey texture) Wira SHK/Shutterstock.com; cover (grass texture) comzeal images/Shutterstock.com; cover (soccer play) Dejan Popovic/Shutterstock.com; p. 5 TandemBranding/Shutterstock.com; p. 7 (top) Alizada Studios/Shutterstock.com; p. 7 (bottom) amorn_me/Shutterstock.com; p. 8 Alex Kravtsov/Shutterstock.com; p. 9 Rui Alexandre Araujo/Shutterstock.com; pp. 11, 22 Puwadol Jaturawutthichai/Shutterstock.com; pp. 13, 25, 27 Vasyl Shulga/Shutterstock.com; p. 15 Vlad1988/Shutterstock.com; p. 17 (top) Yiorgos GR/Shutterstock.com; p. 17 (bottom) daykung/Shutterstock.com; p. 18 wavebreakmedia/Shutterstock.com; p. 19 Master1305/Shutterstock.com; p. 21 A.RICARDO/Shutterstock.com; p. 23 Photo Works/Shutterstock.com; p. 26 alphaspirit.it/Shutterstock.com; p. 29 Monkey Business Images/Shutterstock.com.

Library of Congress Cataloging-in-Publication Data

Names: Martin, Emmett, author.
Title: Positions in soccer / Emmett Martin.
Description: New York : PowerKids Press, 2023. | Series: Positions on the
   team | Includes index.
Identifiers: LCCN 2022002072 (print) | LCCN 2022002073 (ebook) | ISBN
   9781538387153 (library binding) | ISBN 9781538387139 (paperback) | ISBN
   9781538387146 (set) | ISBN 9781538387160 (ebook)
Subjects: LCSH: Soccer–Juvenile literature.
Classification: LCC GV943.25 .M275 2023 (print) | LCC GV943.25 (ebook) |
   DDC 796.334–dc23/eng/20220118
LC record available at https://lccn.loc.gov/2022002072
LC ebook record available at https://lccn.loc.gov/2022002073

Manufactured in the United States of America

CPSIA Compliance Information: Batch #CSPK23. For Further Information contact Rosen Publishing, New York, New York at 1-800-237-9932.

Find us on

CONTENTS

THE BEAUTIFUL GAME

Have you ever heard someone call soccer "the Beautiful Game"? You might wonder why. It could be because soccer is a sport anyone with a ball can play. It could be because soccer unites different people as they root for their favorite team. Or it could be that it's just beautiful to watch the ball soaring through the air, a player racing down the field, and a goalkeeper making the catch before the ball enters the net. These are the moments that bring joy, alarm, and excitement to fans and players alike.

Each soccer team has 11 players on the field. Let's look at every position—from keeper to striker!

GET THE GEAR

All you need is a ball and some friends to play soccer, but it's important to stay safe in a real game. Some pieces of equipment can protect your body. Soccer shoes called cleats can help you keep your footing, and shin pads (or shin guards) can protect your legs from other players' kicks!

THINK FAST!

SOCCER'S OBJECT IS SIMPLE ENOUGH—KICK THE BALL INTO THE NET. BUT GAMES ARE OFTEN LOW SCORING IF EVERYONE IS GOOD AT THEIR JOB.

You might call this game soccer, but people in many countries call it football. Either way, you're talking about the most popular sport in the world!

KEEPER OF THE BALL

A soccer team has ten fielders and one goalkeeper, sometimes called the keeper or goalie. Keepers have one of the hardest jobs on the field, but they have a special rule to help them do it: they can use their hands. In fact, they can use any part of their body to stop a shot on net when they're in the penalty area.

Keepers must have a lot of different skills to stop shots. They need excellent **reflexes**. They need good hands to catch shots or punch them far from the net. They must also be able to roll, throw, or kick the ball **accurately** to teammates.

GLOVES ON

Goalkeepers have a piece of equipment that other players lack: gloves. Gloves help protect fingers from being injured by hard shots. Keepers learn how to stop shots with these heavy gloves and not give up rebounds, which are when the ball bounces away from the keeper and can be shot into the net again.

THINK FAST!
A KEEPER NEEDS TO DECIDE QUICKLY WHETHER TO THROW THE BALL TO A CLOSE TEAMMATE OR **PUNT** IT DOWN THE FIELD.

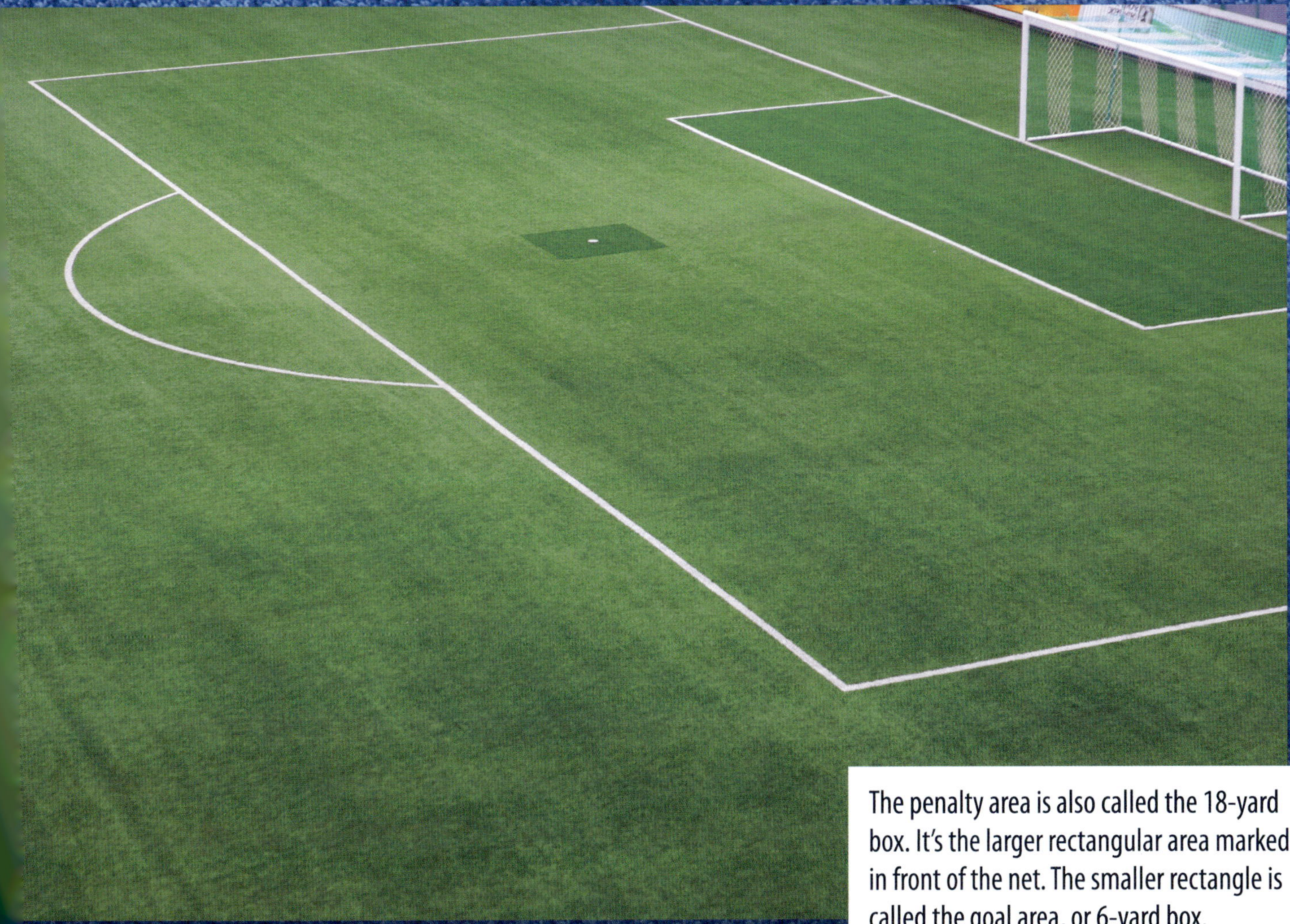

The penalty area is also called the 18-yard box. It's the larger rectangular area marked in front of the net. The smaller rectangle is called the goal area, or 6-yard box.

THREE FIELD POSITIONS

Most positions in soccer besides the goalkeeper are grouped into three categories: forwards, defenders, and midfielders. Forwards mostly play in the offensive zone, trying to score goals on the other team's keeper. They often take passes from other players on their team and score most of the team's goals.

SAME BUT DIFFERENT

Players with the same basic position on a soccer team may play slightly different roles. Coaches decide how best to use their players in different plays and formations that give the team a good balance of offense and defense. After all, teams need to score goals while stopping the other team from scoring too.

Defenders mostly play in the defensive zone in front of their goalkeeper. They make up what's called the back line—the last line of defense trying to stop the other team from getting shots on net.

Midfielders play between forwards and defenders. They provide the link between offense and defense.

THINK FAST!
FORWARDS ARE ALSO CALLED ATTACKERS BECAUSE OF THEIR READY-TO-SCORE OFFENSIVE POSITION NEAR THE GOAL.

Every team has only one goalkeeper on the field. The other 10 players on the field are a mix of defenders, midfielders, and forwards.

WHAT'S A FORMATION?

The number of forwards, midfielders, and defenders a team has on the field depends on their formation. A formation is described by three or four numbers that tell how many different players are in each row across the field. The numbers don't include the goalkeeper.

For example, one of the most common formations in soccer is the 4–4–2, which is four defenders, four midfielders, and two forwards in front of a keeper. This formation offers lots of defensive help to a team's keeper while two forwards are positioned to score. Another formation, the 4–3–3, has three forwards to boost a team's offensive attack.

CHANGING THE BALANCE

Soccer's changing formations have changed the look of the game. A common formation in the late 1800s was the 2-3-5. That's just two defenders, three midfielders, and five forwards. Games back then had more goals because defenses didn't have enough players to stop other teams from scoring. Modern soccer formations, however, usually have more defenders than forwards.

THINK FAST!

A TEAM CAN SWITCH FORMATIONS DURING A GAME DEPENDING ON THEIR CHANGING OFFENSIVE AND DEFENSIVE NEEDS.

SOCCER FORMATIONS

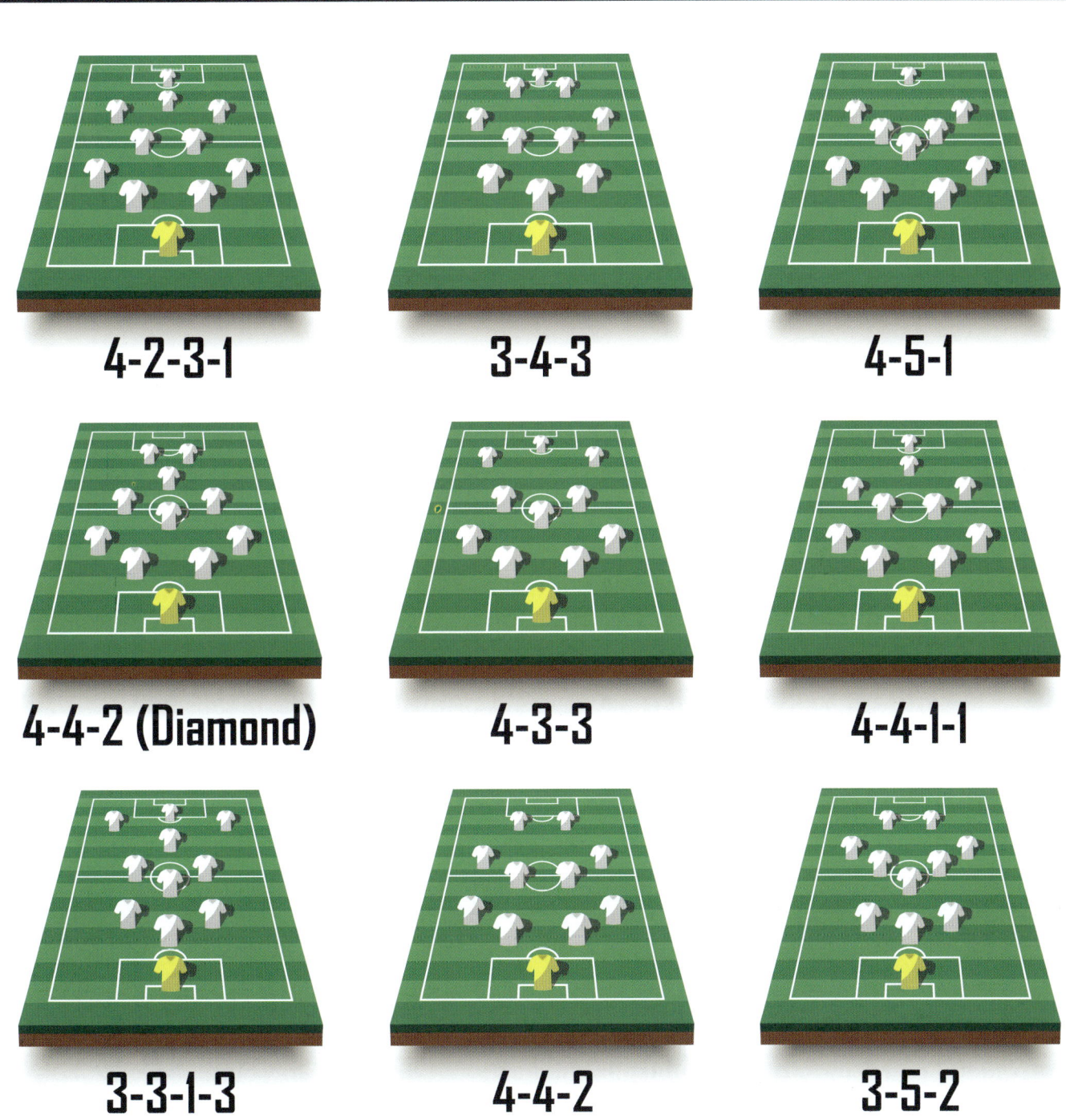

4-2-3-1

3-4-3

4-5-1

4-4-2 (Diamond)

4-3-3

4-4-1-1

3-3-1-3

4-4-2

3-5-2

A formation usually has front, back, and middle sections at least.

BACKBONE OF THE DEFENSE

A soccer team's defense is made up of different kinds of defenders. One main defensive role is called center back (also called central defender). In a four-player defense, the center backs are in the middle of the back line, closest to their own goal. Center backs often have leadership roles, directing other defenders and even midfielders assisting the defense.

Center backs need to be good at tackling, or legally taking the ball away from an opponent without making contact with them. It also helps if center backs are tall, so they can **head** balls away from the net that the opponent may send into the penalty area.

HISTORIC HALF

A center back is sometimes called a center half, but this generally is an old term left over from the old 2-3-5 field formations of the 19th century. The row of three players were called halfbacks, with the center player called the center half. This position shifted back a row in most formations.

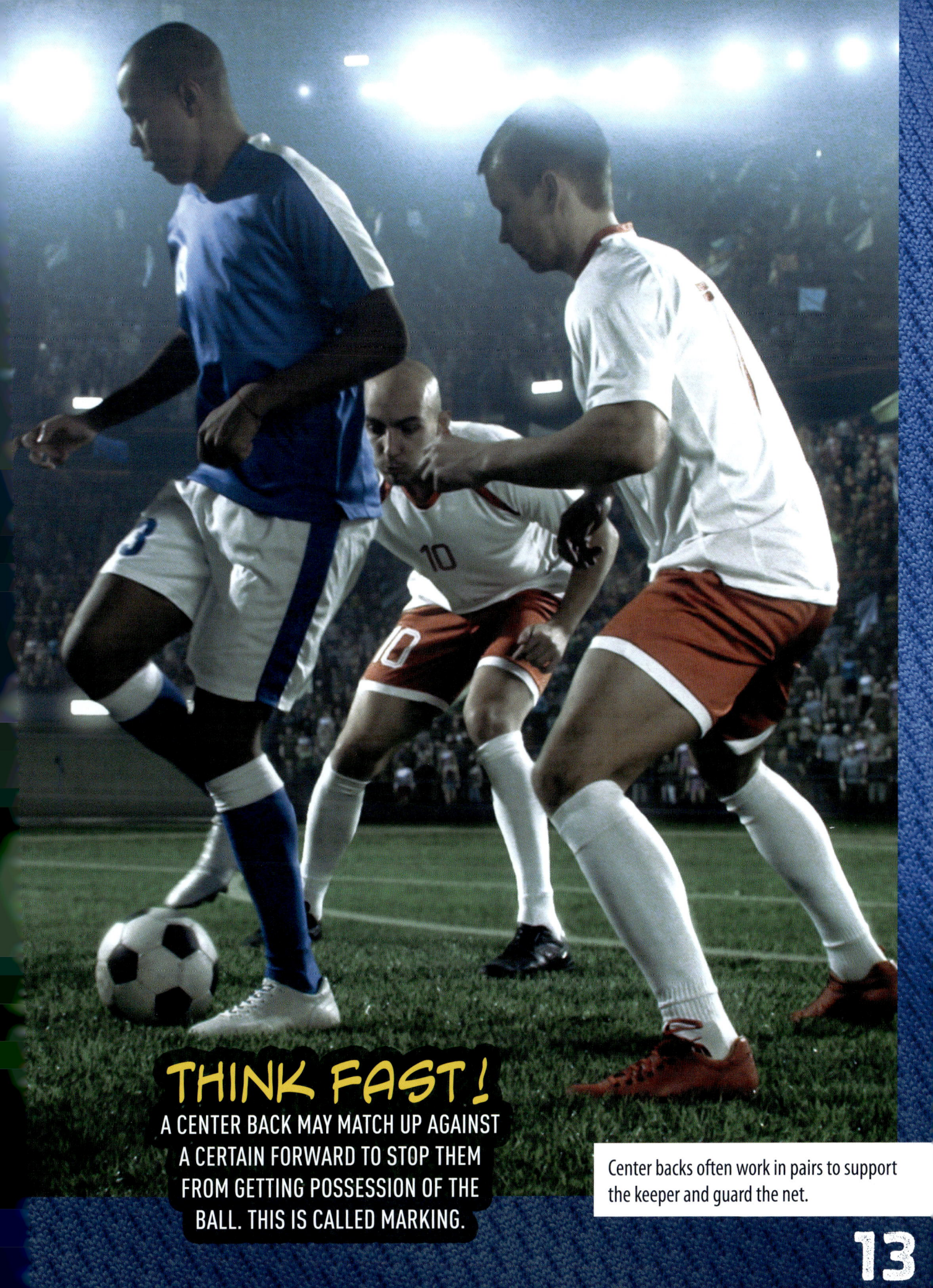

THINK FAST!

A CENTER BACK MAY MATCH UP AGAINST A CERTAIN FORWARD TO STOP THEM FROM GETTING POSSESSION OF THE BALL. THIS IS CALLED MARKING.

Center backs often work in pairs to support the keeper and guard the net.

NOT ON THE SIDELINES

Fullbacks are defensive players that line up near the sidelines (or touchlines). They're usually a bit smaller than center backs but quicker. While they help center backs defend if the ball is moved toward the middle of the field, they also focus on helping their offense get possession of the ball.

Fullbacks often have to mark an offensive player called a **winger**. They must be fast enough to stop a player on the wing, or side, from sending long passes to the center of the field near the goal, which are called crosses. They need to be smart enough to read what their opponent's offense is trying to do.

WINGBACKS

A wingback is the name sometimes given to a defender that plays a much more offensive role than a fullback. You could think of it as a cross between a fullback and a winger. Wingbacks play farther up the field, just behind the midfielders. They're defenders that also support their team's attack.

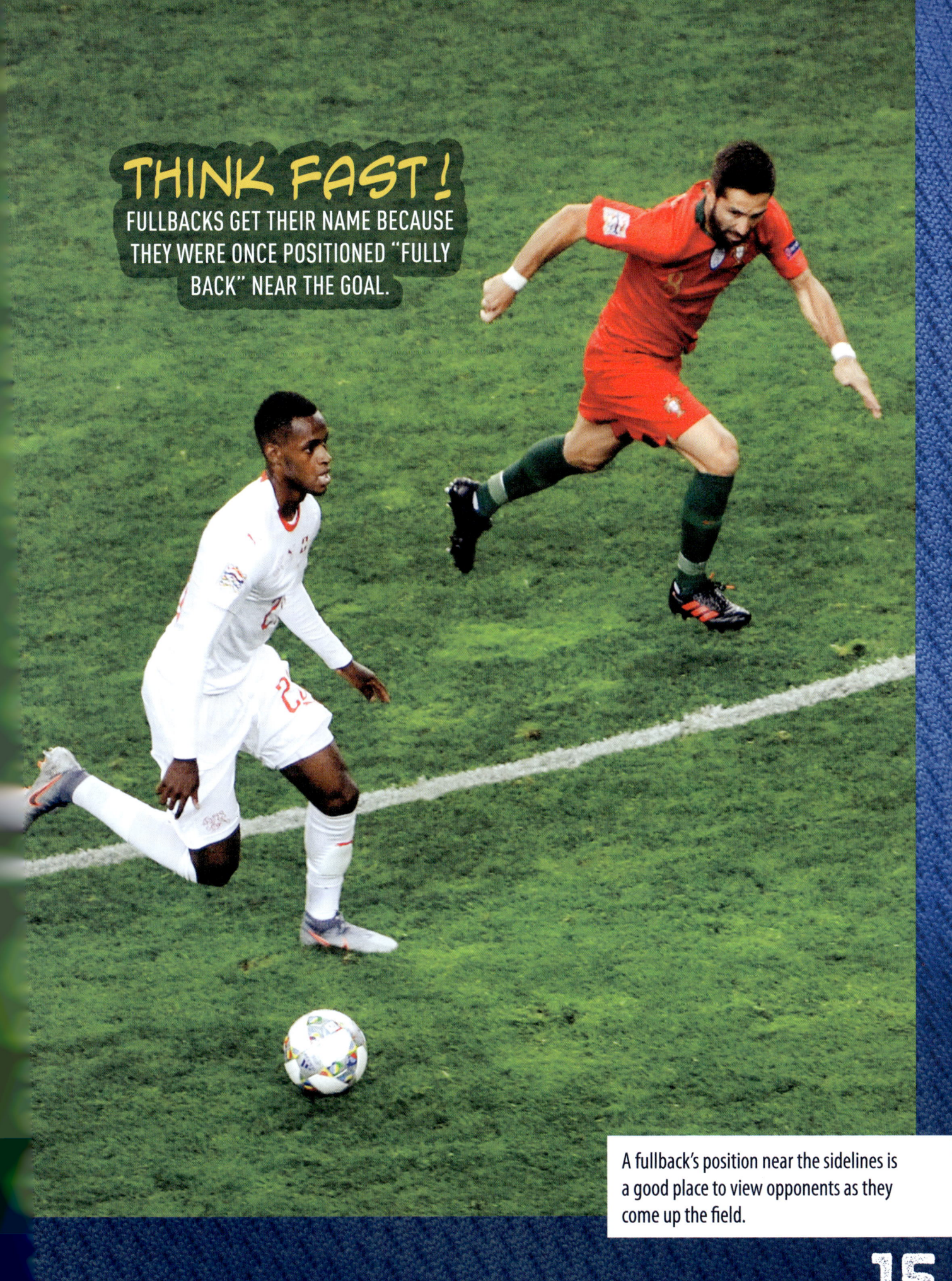

A fullback's position near the sidelines is a good place to view opponents as they come up the field.

NO OFFSIDE!

The offside rule in soccer can sound confusing, but it's essential for all players to understand. Offensive players must stay onside, or make sure at least one of their opponents (besides the keeper) is closer than they are to the net when the ball is passed to them. This means players must make a "run" behind the defense after a ball is sent their way.

Back lines may try to "trap" offensive players by moving upfield to put forwards offside. When an offensive player is offside, the **referee** blows the whistle and gives the ball to the other team.

SWEEPER

One defensive role rarely seen today is the sweeper. The sweeper plays closest to the keeper behind the other defenders, moving around and "sweeping" away the ball if it gets that far. Today, the term is sometimes used to describe a very active defender or the player with the most skill working on the defensive end.

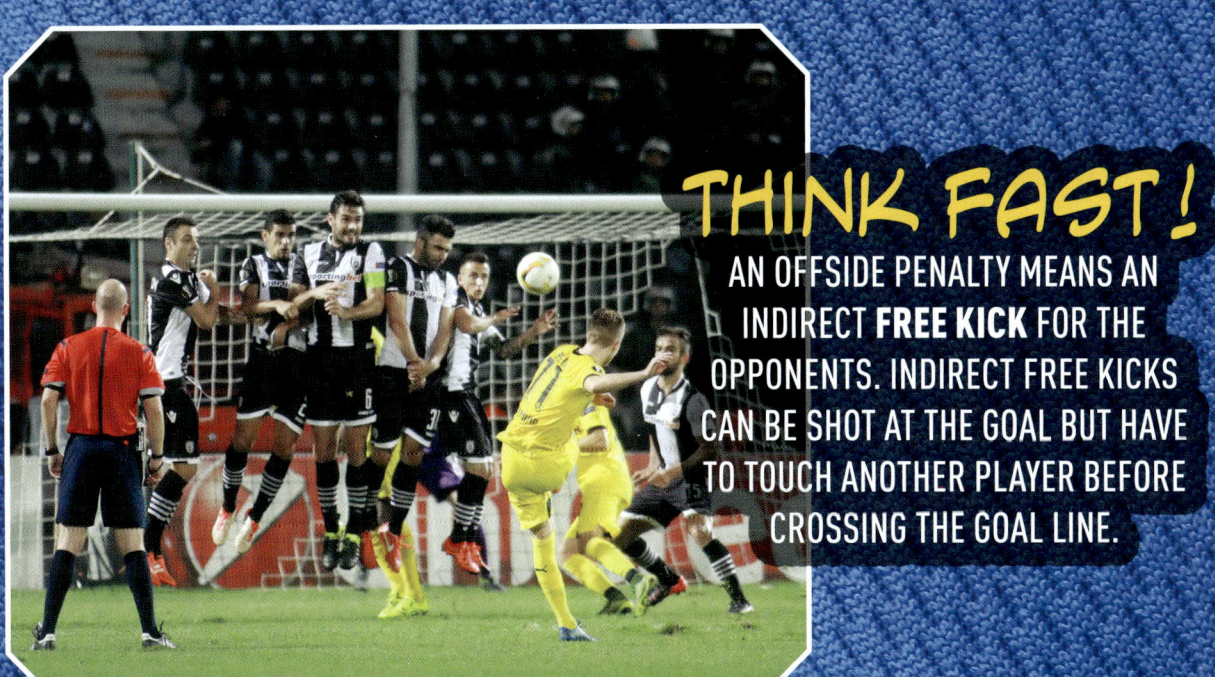

THINK FAST!

AN OFFSIDE PENALTY MEANS AN INDIRECT **FREE KICK** FOR THE OPPONENTS. INDIRECT FREE KICKS CAN BE SHOT AT THE GOAL BUT HAVE TO TOUCH ANOTHER PLAYER BEFORE CROSSING THE GOAL LINE.

Offside rules are in place to make sure an offensive player doesn't just stand near the goal, waiting for the ball.

HOLDING BACK

Midfielders play in the middle of the field. A midfield can have up to five players depending on a team's formation. What these players are called depends on the role they play for their team. The midfielders most focused on defending are called holding or defensive midfielders.

GETTING CARDED

If a defender doesn't tackle cleanly, they could get a card. There are two kinds of cards: a yellow card, which is a warning about playing dangerously, and a red card, which means the offending player has to leave the game immediately. Two yellow cards for one player in a game is the same as a red card. Plus, the carded player's team has to play with just 10 players!

Holding midfielders "hold" their position in front of their defensive back line and try to keep the ball—and opponents—getting any farther down the field. Holding midfielders are good at getting in the way of passes, filling passing lanes in the middle of the field, and tackling with great **precision**.

THINK FAST!

THERE'S AN EVEN MORE **SPECIALIZED** HOLDING MIDFIELDER CALLED A DEEP-LYING PLAYMAKER. THIS PLAYER MOSTLY STAYS IN THE DEFENSIVE MIDFIELD TRYING TO MAKE LONG PASSES TO HELP THEIR TEAM SCORE.

If a defender misses the ball on a tackle, the opponent may get past them. If they hit the other player, the opponent may get a direct free kick, which is an unopposed kick directly shot at the goal.

ACTION IN THE MIDDLE

An attacking midfielder takes a much more offensive role. This player is sometimes called a playmaker because they're expected to lead the offense and make plays happen. They pass the ball to other midfielders and forwards to get it into the opponent's box and get shots on net.

Attacking midfielders need to be skillful with the ball, be able to keep possession in the middle of the field, and feed the ball to others in positions to create offense. Attacking midfielders aren't expected to play defense as much as other midfielders, but they help out when needed.

FROM BOX TO BOX

Central (or center) midfielders have an accurate name. They stay at the center of the field and try to control play. Some central midfielders are called box-to-box midfielders because they run from one end's penalty area to the other, playing both offense and defense. They have great ball control.

THINK FAST !

FAMOUS ATTACKING MIDFIELDERS INCLUDE DIEGO MARADONA AND ZINEDINE ZIDANE.

The best playmakers in soccer, including some attacking midfielders, wear the number 10.

GOING WIDE

Wide midfielders, like central midfielders, play defense and offense. Also called right or left midfielders (or wingers), they play near the sidelines and focus on offense, finding spaces to feed the ball to teammates who can move up the field. Wide midfielders are unselfish, looking for ways to help the team as a whole, rather than getting a goal on their own. And on defense, they put pressure on outside opponents and cut off passing lanes.

READY TO GO

Wide midfielders play on the sidelines when their team is in possession, so they can see the field and decide what to do. When their team loses possession, they can run infield to help defend. Common formations that include wide midfielders are the 4–4–2, the 4–4–1–1, and the 4–5–1.

4-4-2

4-4-1-1

4-5-1

A wide midfielder must be an excellent dribbler, using their feet to shield the ball with skillful footwork. These players are often up against one or two opponents, so ball-handling skills are essential.

THINK FAST!
WIDE MIDFIELDERS NEED TO PUT THEMSELVES INTO A POSITION TO SERVE UP CROSSES TO THEIR TEAMMATES.

David Beckham, above, is perhaps the most famous wide midfielder in the world even though he's retired from the game.

MOVING FORWARD

You might think forwards aren't as **athletic** as other soccer players. After all, these players don't seem to move around the field as much as their teammates do. Instead, they wait for chances to score goals. But they do move—a lot—as they use their skills to get the ball past defenders and keepers. Forwards score most often on their team.

The center forward plays the central position for the forwards. They often have size and strength as well as the height to receive a pass and head the ball into the goal. Many center forwards play in front of the attacking midfielders and do most of the ball handling outside the penalty area.

STRIKERS

Sometimes forwards are called strikers. A striker is also the name for the player positioned closest to the opponent's goal. This player must take passes from teammates and get accurate shots past the keeper. Strikers are fast and able to keep possession of the ball while fighting off multiple defenders.

THINK FAST!

CENTER FORWARDS ARE OFTEN THE FIRST ATTACKER ON THEIR TEAM TO RUN INTO THE PENALTY AREA.

Center forwards score many of their goals with their head!

A wing forward plays to the left or the right of the center forward. Their main job is to dribble the ball up the field and pass to the center forward. Wing forwards may shoot on goal if they have a clean shot, though.

Some teams use a forward called a second forward or second striker (also deep-lying forward) between the midfield and the center forward. This player creates scoring opportunities for other forwards.

PENALTY KICKS

When a foul is called on the defense in the penalty area, the team on offense gets a penalty kick. This is a shot on goal with just the keeper defending the net. Strikers often take penalties and need to stay calm and trick the keeper with their shots. Could you take the pressure?

Talented forwards can make contact with the ball using their head and direct it into the net from anywhere inside the box. They're often called upon to make penalty kicks too.

Before a penalty kick, the ball is placed on the penalty mark on the field, which is 12 yards (11 m) in front of the goal line. All players except the keeper and kicker must stay beyond the penalty arc until the kicker touches the ball.

SO MUCH MORE

There are even *more* specialized positions among defenders, midfielders, and forwards! Keep reading to learn more. And don't forget to watch games too. You'll see that teams have different styles of play.

On offense, some teams like to make a lot of passes before finding a weakness in the defense and going for the goal. This is called indirect attack. Quickly moving the ball up the field to score is called direct attack. On defense, the two main styles of play are a zone defense and a marking defense (or person-to-person defense). Soccer is truly "the Beautiful Game"!

THE COACH KNOWS

Coaches are often called managers in soccer, but no matter what you call them, you should pay attention to them! Coaches can teach you lots of things to make you better at soccer, like **strategy**. They can also help you find your perfect position on the field based on your special skills.

THE STYLE CALLED TOTAL FOOTBALL MEANS ANY PLAYER CAN TAKE THE POSITION OF ANY OTHER PLAYER ON THE TEAM. THAT MEANS EVERY PLAYER MUST BE GOOD AT EVERY POSITION TO BE READY TO SWITCH!

Soccer coaches have a lot of jobs. Training players and planning strategies are just two of them.

GLOSSARY

accurately: In a way that is free of mistakes or able to hit a target.

athletic: Active in sports or exercises or strong and muscular.

free kick: A kick taken by a player without opposition to start play after an opponent has committed a foul.

head: To play the ball with the forehead, whether trying to clear it, pass it, or shoot at the goal.

precision: The quality of being exact or accurate.

punt: A kick that a player makes by dropping a ball and kicking it before it touches the ground.

referee: An official who makes sure players follow the rules.

reflex: A fast reaction done without thinking.

specialized: Adapted to focus on a certain purpose.

strategy: A plan of action to achieve a goal.

winger: A soccer player who is not a defender who plays on the left or right sides of the field. A winger can be a left or right midfielder, left or right attacking midfielder, or left or right forward.

FOR MORE INFORMATION

BOOKS

Dufresne, Emilie. *Soccer*. New York, NY: Kidhaven Publishing, 2020.

Hammelef, Danielle S. *First Source to Soccer: Rules, Equipment, and Key Playing Tips*. North Mankato, MN: Capstone Press, 2018.

Mikoley, Kate. *Soccer: Stats, Facts, and Figures*. New York, NY: Gareth Stevens Publishing, 2018.

WEBSITES

Soccer Football
www.ducksters.com/sports/soccer.php
Find lots of links to explanations of the many aspects of this beautiful game.

Soccer Positions: A Complete Guide
yoursoccerhome.com/soccer-positions-a-complete-and-easy-to-understand-guide/
There's more to learn about each position of soccer. This site has the answers.

INDEX